I wish I had a better title for this

Sameen Siddiqui

BookLeaf
Publishing

India | USA | UK

I wish I had a better title for this © 2022

Sameen Siddiqui

All rights reserved.

No part of this publication may be reproduced, stored in a retrieval system, or transmitted, in any form or by any means, electronic, mechanical, photocopying, recording or otherwise, without the prior written permission of the presenters.

Sameen Siddiqui asserts the moral right to be identified as author of this work.

Presentation by *BookLeaf Publishing*

Web: www.bookleafpub.com

E-mail: info@bookleafpub.com

ISBN: 978-93-5761-170-1

First edition 2022

DEDICATION

To those whom I trust and love beyond what any dedication could capture. I hope you know I am immensely grateful for your presence in my life. To SA, MA and I.H.

ACKNOWLEDGEMENT

First and foremost, all success and goodness is from Allah (swt). I thank Him for the countless blessings bestowed upon me; the ability to feel, to think, to write and the opportunity to share - to name a few.

Next, I would never have had the courage to share any of my work if it were not for my phenomenally supportive friends. Thank you for being the inspiration behind many pieces, my trusted sounding boards and for encouraging me the way you all always do.

PREFACE

Thank you for picking up my book!

This collection of poetry has been more than six years in the making. I started writing spoken word during the first year of university. A friend sent me a TEDtalk by Sarah Kay in which she talks about her journey of spoken word and performs a piece titled 'B'. It's an eighteen minute video, and that was all it took for me to fall in love not only with Sarah Kay's work, but the concept of spoken word itself. I found myself writing poetry as a way to deal with my experiences, but soon realised it wasn't enough to just write it. I wanted to share it, in fact I wanted to perform it. What started as a lime green notebook in which I wrote at every opportunity, usually sat somewhere along the River Thames, is now the book in your hands,

In the last six years, I have filled several more notebooks with poetry. Even with the increasing use of technology, I always find myself drawn to pen and paper when trying to make sense of either what is happening around me or going on inside me.

I struggled when it came to ordering the poems for this book, especially because there is no single theme and I cannot preface each piece like I might have done at an open-mic with a little spiel about its origins. So instead, I'm relying on footnotes and subheadings to provide you with some context.

The order I've gone with is one which makes sense in my head. It's not a narrative, nor are the pieces linked, but they **are** intentionally ordered to create a flow which feels natural. I hope you enjoy it.

I wish I had a better title for this

"I wish I had a better title for this"
because so much has happened, but hearing the
question - If you were to write the story of your
life, what would the title be? - makes my mind
go blank.
Because all of a sudden I feel I've never done
anything significant,
Or significant enough to warrant a title.
I *am* only 23 so I guess that's an excuse, I
haven't had much time to do much at all.
If I had to come up with a title, I guess I'd say
"somehow flying through without even knowing
how to walk"
As far as I know, it feels like I only know how to
crawl
and isn't it supposed to be walk, then run, then
fly
but I'm flying
Somehow I'm going to be a doctor next year
Dealing with the aftermath of COVID in just
eighteen months
And yet I still have to google blood pressure
management every time.

I'm a family person, a friend person, an everyone
person
a there-to-help, a there-to-listen person
Somehow without even knowing what makes
me a person

So yeah, I wish I knew more
I wish I had more direction
I wish I cared less about the opinions of others
and I wish I had a better title - than this one.

The Fig Tree

Inspired by Sylvia Plath's 'The Bell Jar'

I want to immerse myself in my work
think of nothing else
live among my books - and learn.
Learn as much as I can about the world that I
live in
but also learn as best as I can about the career I'd
like to live with
Be a good doctor - really make a difference
to every single one of my patients.

Yet, I also just want to abandon books
there's only so much to be gained
from ink printed on pages
I'd rather ink my own pages
travel as much as I can
and write my own stories
taking inspiration from everyone I meet and
their own journeys
every country, every place
has so much history
and I'd like to learn from it all by being there
I cannot see what's out there if I keep sitting in
here

Yet, all I want to do is sit here.
Sorry, I lied -
all I want to do is lie here
in my bed, away from this world that keeps on
moving
and just take a break
   - pause
         - breathe
               - sleep.

And yet, if I sleep my life away
how will I live?
Start to make reality this dream that was planted
so long ago
of a husband, children, my own home?
To have someone who understands me
completely,
and accepts me for me
and children - the joy that they would bring
would I want to deprive myself of them?

So many questions, so many paths
as I lay there under the fig tree
trying to pick one
but all I seem to be doing
is watching the fallen ones rot and decay
turning soft, brown, and then disintegrate-ing
and the most frustrating part of it all

is I don't even like figs
so how can I want so many of them?

Superpowers

I'm going to let you in
on an age old secret
that I've discovered a long while ago
but deciphered only very recently
and that is, are you ready? -
Marriage gives you superpowers.
Marriage makes you a superwoman.

And don't we all want to be superwomen?
Or at least we ought to want to be
That is why our greatest aspirations
should always, and exclusively, be
Marriage.

Now, even though it's supposed to be a secret
My mother and aunt and all the elders
have somehow let it slip
and given my inclination to share, I'd like to
share the story of this secret with you
It's not really a story, more like a broken record
but I'm sure you'll catch on...

Mum, can I pierce my nose?
When you're married.
Can I dye my hair?

When you're married.
I want to travel the world!
When you're married.
Can I start a charity?
When you're married.
What about my own business?
When you're married.

So naturally, it follows right?
Can I start living, be a better me?
I suppose I can, when I'm married.
So that's it folks,
we had it all wrong
There we were, mistaken, delusional
thinking that we needed dedication
and perseverance
expecting to shed blood, sweat and tears
to achieve our goals
when all we really need
is to sign a piece of paper
so that we can inherit the superpowers
which will magically fulfil our dreams
Seems almost foolish now doesn't it
to ever have thought otherwise!

But then when things go wrong,
it's always just 'so unfortunate'
or rather, it's us - the younger generation
who don't know how to fix up

or hold relationships down
we want the quick fix or just to throw broken
things away
yet we're forced to throw broken dreams away
because what did they expect?
when they placed those expect-ations
on such a fragile matter
a marriage was never going to be able to bear
the weight
of a young woman's life's worth of dreams
all waiting, reliant on marriage to set them free.

It seems to me so many of us
have it the wrong way around
Marriage is a part of life
A beautiful part which brings joy and love and
happiness
and yet, it is still just a part of life
it should not be the start of life
and it's considered near blasphemy for me to say
this out loud
but surely marriage is not the main aim of life?

I know it's supposed to be my life's greatest
dream
and when I'm not dreaming that dream anymore
It's like I have insomnia
I'll drink a whole lot of coffee
which brings with it plenty of clarity

reminding me of all the phrases I've heard far
too often
"Oh you're so tall, you'll never find a man"
As if that was her life's plan, or
"you can't wear heels, you'll intimidate him"
because the way she feels about herself or
the way she'd like to look
is worth far, far less
than his precious ego.

How unsettling, that this is not unusual or
strange
in fact, it's in everyday vernacular
and something we're expected to have accepted
and perhaps I'm missing a point somewhere
but I'm not willing to wait until my title changes
from Miss to Mrs
to live out my dreams
and have goals beyond what my perfect wedding
will look like.

Stuck

If they knew the things you do,
the extent you go to every night,
just to hide the pain inside,
Would they change their mind?
Let go of the stigmas once and for all?

I don't think so, I don't think they would
because their thoughts and the way they think
is ingrained in them, a part of their upbringing
and what am I, a 19-year-old going to do
to change their 50-something years of childhood
moulded by over a 100-odd years of culture?

All it will end in is heartbreak and misery
for all those involved, but especially me
because I will never be able to take back those
words
or restore their opinions of who they thought I
was
so I put my mask on
and go back to being their loved little girl.

Shell

*Inspired by a tiny basket of shells that I keep on
my bedside table. They were a gift from a friend,
who asked her brother to bring them back from a
trip to Dover, because she knows how much I
like the seaside and water..*

In those moments, when we are
lost and unrecognisable
when we are mere shells of
who we used to be,
who we used to think we were,
and who we thought we were supposed to be,
when our perception of us is disrupted
like ripples ripping through
our reflections in the still waves of yesterday
I want to remind you,
that we'll be okay
In fact, we'll be better than okay
because when there's nothing
left but the shells of past us
we have the power to create
who we want to be
fix our own perceptions
and then finally,
be 100% us.

choosing happy

Today I won't be sad
Today I choose happy
I stand there looking into this hotel mirror
with luggage strewn on the floor beside me
and behind me
and despite four lights being on, the
lighting is shitty
I cannot tell if my makeup is done right
or my foundation blended
I look at the unmade bed with the
all white once-crisp bed linen
and think of whether they've ever
accidentally dyed anything pink or blue or grey
I look back at the new black linen dress I'm
wearing
I can still see the tag I've just taken off
on the side table
Alongside it I notice my hairband
It reminds me that my hair is still undone
Messy but at least untangled since
I combed it through this morning
I still have to wear my hijab,
haven't gotten round to that yet
I'll do it soon, I think, I have a few minutes to
spare

Before I head down to the orangerie
where breakfast is served
where people await
I look back to my dress and how the ties at the
back are too tight
and I realise I don't like the way it fits
I look fat
Then I think, well that's probably because I am
fa-- stop.
Body positivity - I remind myself
Remember today, I choose happy.
So I force myself to smile,
smile so wide because I'm choosing happy
till my eyes start watering
and suddenly I'm crying
I remind myself that I chose happy
so these must be happy tears
And I rush downstairs
not waiting for the lift
No time to slow down or be still
So I happily run down the stairs
praying my mascara won't smudge
from all the happy tears there have been this
morning
I walk into the bright room
where there are orange trees and fresh orange
juice
with a bright smile plastered on my face
I keep a loop playing in my head

I choose happy, I choose happy, I choose happy
And make a comment about whether the orange
juice
is from the oranges from the orange trees
I ask about if they slept well and aren't we all
excited (!)
They talk about ...
                    ...something
Somehow I cannot hear them
They're now far away, and their voices are
fading
I look around and they're laughing
so I join in too - I think
And that's it, that's the start of my happy day

I felt like maybe even though I chose it,
happy did not want me today.

panic

there is a weight on my chest
it's metaphorical, but with literal effects
because it's so very hard to breathe
I can't lift my ribs far enough
to even allow a trickle of air through
yet my heart is pounding away
as if it's trying to push this weight
off, from the inside out
forgetting there's a wall in between
and that it hurts with every beat
now I'm restless
pacing from one place to another
never staying still long enough
for others to recognise my situation
but each step is uncertain
stopping me from moving
preventing me from taking the next one
ironic because my heart is racing
but if you saw me now
you'd see me sat on a bench
enjoying this beautiful day
and the warm weather we're blessed with
but what good is the wind in my hijab
if there's no air in my lungs?
this feeling is terrifying

because I don't know what's happening
or why it is that
this metaphorical weight is
suffocating me so literally

Stars

Growing up in London, seeing stars was rare.
Still, it became one of my favourite things to do.

Stars.
Spectacularly shining
they uncover themselves at night
and if you're not under London's
polluted sky
then they'll capture your eye
leaving you in awe
of their tremendous beauty
the symbol of hope
for those lost loved ones
as they look down upon us
stumbling on in this world
they align almost perfectly
when the perfect two meet
the picture of romance
when lovers stargaze
the picture of love
as friends lie and make
up their own constellations
with their own spin on the stories
of how they got there
the perfect picture

every time
with their beauty unanimously agreed upon
by all those who have cast their eye
Yet, in actual fact, stars are burning
nearing their end
with every passing night
and unbeknownst to us
one is lost, every damn night
I wish I could save one's life
in thanks for the many many times
I've looked up at the sky
and melted into the stars
and for that second, nothing else mattered at all
I want one more star to live
so I could embody their spirit
of beauty
tonight, I'll burn in place of them
losing me instead of the flickering
light in the night sky
unbeknown to most, I'll be gone by the time
morning comes around
and it'll be okay
because in sunlight
stars are meant to fade away.

trying

today I tried
tried to smile and laugh and talk
be productive and part of it all
dug deep within my mind
amongst the dirty brown boxes
messily sellotaped shut
blowing the dust of the top
only for it to fall back into my face
rubbing my ears
until the tears threatened to spill
scrambled on my hands and knees
to manage the mess
until my skin was scratched and bruised
threatening to rip
I looked as well as I could
and found some remnants of my past self

today I tried to be the old me
or rather I should say the young me
the happy me
the well me
the me that could take on the world
deflecting any negativity that dared to come my
way
the me that was excited and passionate

about so many things in life
the me who was happy to be alive

and in my head,
before I could get ahead of myself
I reminded myself to ration this version of me
make her last longer, for an extra few days
so that the benefit of my time spent searching
in this dusty attic for her
wouldn't be so short lived

today I tried
tried to let go
not weigh myself down
with the dark thoughts
I never run out of
I accepted the day for what it was
and went about trying to make it a little bit better

today I tried to be the sky
instead of the cloud
yet I found that I was neither
I was in fact the child underneath the
grey cloud without an umbrella

today I tried
and today I failed
just like every other day.

Reconciliation

Here I am, attempting to understand,
what it means to reconcile;
Reconciliation is the restoration
of friendly relations
or making compatible
views and beliefs with one another

For quite some time, I've been trying to figure
out
who I am and how I'd define this person I've
become
I'm this morphed, tangled version
of who I once was and who I thought I had to be
my mask no longer distinct from my skin
much like pia mater and the brain
the two are linked, intimate-ly.

When the darkness first fell
and engulfed me entirely
I knew who I was, or at least I thought I did
so that version continued to live on the outside
Became my mask, the animated screen I lived
behind
unable to scream, or shout, or cry

As the real me hid inside, having been robbed dry
of any happiness that once ran in those veins of mine
Now, almost eight years on
I have started to question what had become routine
am I who I say I am, or am I as I feel?
And was there ever a real me?
Is anyone really them at the age of thirteen?

I think now, I never knew who I was,
there never was a whole me
and this darkness spared me no light
no mercy to even try
and grow, develop, into a person that is whole
more confused now than ever before
I'm trying to distinguish between who I am and what I show
my skin is my mask
and my mask is my skin
this darkness is in my mind
and my mind is the dark-est place I know.

So here I am, attempting to reconcile
the two versions of me
that until now had lived separately
Friends, and yet, enemies
never co-existing peacefully

I'm begging the two of you, please
be compatible
be friendly.

The real you

Written for my friend when we were just becoming friends. A way for me to open up a conversation I wasn't sure how to approach

I want to say the real you is strong & funny &
witty and & so completely
Unaware of herself
But I can't, that would take it too far
Because if you don't know the real you
Then how can I claim to?

To be fair, self hatred is a bitch
You and I both know that so well
She can tell us things we don't want to hear
Don't want to believe
Don't want to be true
And yet we do, just that
We believe her and every word that flies out of
her mouth
A high speed bullet created to damage
But we're still standing, so it's clearly not
managed

Believe me I know
I know your shell is comfortable

Just like my mask is
Even I forget to take it off some nights
Not caring about being able to breathe
Because the mask makes everything better
Like your shell makes everything safer

I'm sorry that your safety blanket is ablaze
And damn, I'm even more sorry that I'm to
blame
But know that through the foggy smoke of this
fire
The real you will emerge, all the more wiser

I don't know what you see when you stand in
front of the mirror
But from where I stand, this is my view
I see you
Beautiful but unaware
Strong but unaware
Kind & funny & yet, still, unaware
Maybe it's because of the fire around you
And your mirror is stained with soot
Your lungs heavy with smoke
And your heart heavy with fear
That anything you might do
Would leave you open to scrutiny.

I know you're scared, terrified in fact
To be honest, I am too – every day, every hour

But I am not afraid of standing here
Relaying the parts of you I see
And I will continue to do so relentlessly
Until you no longer need others to see
The very things which amaze me.

Remembering

Remember
Remember everything
Don't forget
The battles you fought
On your own at fourteen
The tears you cried
All alone at sixteen
Remember the goodbyes you said
You really meant, at eighteen

Remember everything
Remember the good times
Back when you were ten
Or even better, back at home
Around the age of seven
When you played in the sun
And came back scratched and bruised
Into the arms of your mother
Who wiped your tears and washed your wounds
Yes, battle wounds – against the elements
With that horrible soap you hated
Remember the sting of Dettol*?
But it was supposed to be good for you
Then think of this sting
Maybe this will be good for you

Or at least, it isn't going to kill you

Remember those adverts on TV
Not only Dettol, but that damn Fair and Lovely*
Remember that feeling of fear as you realised
That playing in the sun might not be all nice
Because it would make you ugly, or un-lovely
Yet you did it anyway
Remember how you understood better as a child
That what others say isn't all the important
Nor is it always right
Fair is lovely, and so is dark
Your beauty is defined by your character

Remember everything
Remember your favourite characters as a kid
Watching Cartoon Network like an addict
Remember that old house with strange things
Foster's home for imaginary friends
How Bloo didn't leave so long as Mac was there
Remember you'll be okay
There's always someone who cares

Remember everything
Don't forget
Don't forget where you're from
Don't forget what makes you – you
You might not know exactly who you are
But don't ever stop trying to discover you

Remember everything
And don't forget
One day, you'll make it through

*Dettol is an antiseptic disinfectant cleaning
brand, very popular when I was growing up.
*Fair & Lovely is an Indian skin-lightening
cosmetic product, the advertisements for which
were relentless.

Nana

*In Urdu, Nana means Grandad. I never met
mine.*

If he were here today
Would I be here today?
Writing these words
Rearranging the letters in this way
Would I be able to talk to him?
To tell him?
Would I need to tell him?
Or would he just know, be able to see right
through
the facade I've put on
for so damn long now
Would it have even taken this long?
Maybe he would have stopped it earlier
Maybe he would have helped me
But maybe he would have been hurt
to know this girl he loved so much
Was feeling so unloved
Would he have loved me so much?
I wish I could have known
Known all this, but also just
Known him.

The world is a terrible place and I don't know how to navigate it.

I wrote this piece in the middle of the first lockdown.

It feels insensitive to be celebrating
It feels 'un-woke' to feel my losses
of going out and seeing friends,
of studying in a café,
of being back at placement with my flatmates
of praying taraweeh* in that primary school
music room
of sharing iftar* with the neighbourhood
of celebrating Eid properly.
This year has been overwhelming, to say the
least
And I'm struggling to be happy.

I think it's probably more accurate to say
That it's the privilege of being happy which isn't
sitting well me
– and no, I haven't missed the irony.
Especially with nowhere to go,

I walk around the house with it weighing heavy
over me
A constant reminder to be constantly reminding
myself
Of all the terrible current affairs
And if I'm not thinking about all the injustice
consciously, constantly,
Then I'm being complicit in the face of
oppression
Silencing voices which ought to be heard.

I try to be kinder to myself, take a step back and
Remind myself that trials which bring me, and
us collectively, closer to Allah,
Are in fact blessings; and that
اِنَّ مَعَ ٱلْعُسْرِ يُسْرًا
Truly, after every hardship there is ease
[Qur'an 94:5]
I allow myself the gratitude and hope that these
thoughts bring
I struggle however, to allow myself any
happiness
How could I possibly be somewhere even close
to being okay,
When life as I knew it — is disintegrating.

The weight lifts, only in the little moments,
When I'm in sujood*
When I'm petting my cat

When I'm running outside
It doubles down straight after though, and my
heart feels even heavier than before
Heavy with guilt, because I can run outside
safely
When Ahmaud Arbery could not.
Because I can find moments of respite when
there are those who cannot.

Heavy also with sadness for all those people
who are hurting, with loved ones currently
fighting or already lost to COVID-19
Or hurting for reasons related to the pandemic–
who can't escape domestic or child abuse
because we're in lockdown
who are struggling to make ends meet and feed
themselves and their families
who are struggling with being away from their
families because they are healthcare workers and
at high risk of catching and transmitting this
virus
who aren't going to be finding the 'silver
linings' of this lockdown
who are struggling with managing their mental
health amidst all this chaos

It also hard to celebrate, knowing there are so
many suffering

At the hands of the Indian government and
general population
When police brutality takes on a difference face,
and is actively involved
In the ethnic cleansing of Muslims nationally
The venomous thoughts are so deeply ingrained
in them
It's terrifying to see just how openly they are
able to murder.
No world leaders are speaking out, no one seems
to care
Nothing was done when there were lynchings
and hate-crimes
And now, with evidence of detention centres [or
as we've learnt about them, concentration
camps] and dehumanization of an entire
population
Still nothing is done.

I don't know what a post-COVID world will
look like
I have no idea what the long-term ramifications
of this disease will be
I don't know if, and when, persecution will stop
I don't know whether things will ever improve

The world has changed, and it's a scary place
right now

COVID is indiscriminate, and it has taken so
many lives already
It has draped the world with this curtain of pain
and uncertainty
Now, more than ever, there is a rise in
hate-crimes and greater awareness of police
brutality
Awareness, not incidence - and so any sense of
justice is only proportional to the level of public
outrage generated

All this without even mentioning
the ongoing war in Syria
the lockdown as the latest addition to decades of
oppression in Kashmir
the inhumane persecution in Rohingya
the refugee crisis worldwide
the thousands who die hungry and alone
or the upcoming post-COVID financial and
mental health crises.

The world is a terrible place, and I don't know
how to navigate it.
I'm trying to be kind to myself and find ways to
be accepting of this.
To allow myself the time and space to feel
overwhelmed
But also to allow myself the gratitude, hope and
moments of happiness

Because I'm fortunate to have them, and it
would be remiss of me to ignore them.

*taraweeh — additional ritual prayers
performed at night during Ramadan, often in
congregation
*iftar — evening meal, eaten at sunset when fast
ends
*sujood — prostration towards the Holy Kaaba,
part of the daily prayers

Not So Different

You and I we're not so different
and yet we're worlds apart
I cried today, my tears a river
and so did you
except yours were the red sea.

These senseless acts
these atrocities
the never ending calamities
it feels like there is nothing to be said
never the right words
because they could never drown out
the pain and fear
that you feel every day

the pain I feel for you, you - my family
my brothers and sisters in humanity
across the world
and the greater pain you feel
burying yours.

I pray through this pain comes strength and
reward
I pray your pain is not in vain
my heart is broken
but yours must be shattered

You and I - we're not so different
except between the two of us
it is I who is alive.

Apologies

Times like this I want to run away
Hide my tear stricken face
Ashamed to be a part of the world
Where a celebrity's date gets more airtime
than those truly suffering
Even more than that
I am ashamed to be a part of those
'blissfully ignorant'
Unaware of the tragedies of the day
Yet ignorance is not bliss
I refuse for it to be
Because those who go through horror
on a daily basis are surely not in bliss
Me not knowing, doesn't help in any way.

I read an article today on a potential war crime
But what good is that when no one will do the
time?
A refugee centre was bombed today
Taking away what little they have salvaged,
taking away their courageous attempted at
rebuilding
their lives, all taken away, for the sake of it.
My heart bleeds for them, and yet that's nothing
in comparison

to the blood they have shed
the tears they have cried
the lives they have lost
and yet they continue to fight

They are the brave warriors
those who deserve a legacy
in fact they deserve much more than that
they deserve an eternity
in heaven with no further fears
having been reunited with their loved ones
and I have no doubt that they will
for our Rabb does no injustice
But for now they're in pain
Humans, like you and I,
being denied every possible human right
Yet I sit there, ignorant
too cowardly to turn on the news
In fear of the new horrors the day had brought
as if reading a newspaper or watching a
broadcast
Could give me even a little insight
into the harshness of their lives
Their dismembered body parts lie
Scattered in the ground as if to remind
us that it is in fact them who pay the price
of a war in which they took no part
children born into this life
with no choice but to try and survive.

Although this means very little, I know,
to all of you who suffer, I apologise
I apologise for the way you have been treated
For the way I often, too often, turned a blind eye
I apologise that there's not much I can do
to help ease your plight
But know that a beautiful future awaits
one beyond our imaginations
For verily, with hardship comes ease,
and our Rabb is going to grant you all you
deserve and more
You shall have a better life
But until then, I'm afraid all I can do is just
apologise.

Grenfell

So I've sat down to write today
Not entirely sure what I'm trying to say
Not entirely sure whether I'm writing
To the people, for the people, from the people
Who were affected by the fire
What right do I even have anyway?
To write on their behalf
As if I could ever imagine
Even half their pain
Yet all this seems so surreal
That this tragedy, travesty, crime
Which should not have occurred
Is now the source of my inspiration today
I guess all I am trying to say
Is that I wish I could capture
Poetically
Beautifully
Perhaps even provocatively
What they went through,
that devastating night last Ramadan
And that angers me the most
Because there is no bloody way
No way to do this poetically
No way to do it justice

Because beautiful words and eloquent metaphors
are not enough
They could never capture what they felt
What was a real, raw, living nightmare
Adults, children, the entire community
Scarred forever by this tragedy
I have no other way, no other words
But to say I'm sorry, for all that you've suffered
To say I pray for all those who burned
Who have been through hell and can now rest in
heaven
To say I wish things could have ended
differently
To say I wish things could have started
differently
That this could have been yet another accidental
fire
Well contained in a kitchen corner
And that it was not because of the rich-poor
division
That your lives mattered more than the rich
man's vision
Flammable cladding - what the hell were they
thinking?
But God knows exactly what you were thinking
And the pain you suffered
And those who survived are still suffering
The battles that are still being fought
With the only solace in the fact that

Allah (swt) is Al-Adl*, The Just
And that no single act will go unnoticed
For all these burdens you are bearing
I promise you Grenfell, you will have your
justice.

*In Islam, Allah (swt) has 99 blessed name, each
associated with a particular attribute. Al-Adl
stands for The Just, meaning: The one who
rectifies and sets matters straight in a just and
equitable manner. [Taken from myislam.org]*

Gun control

How are you still talking about gun possession
instead of gun control?
How are you still talking as if seventeen lives
were not just taken?
How are you talking as if eighteen school
shootings
have not happened in 2018 alone?
How are you still talking as if you know better
than those who saw their friends die
those who heard their classmates scream -
terrified
How is this something that still happens today?
How are you someone who's still relevant today?
How dare you bring more guns into the picture,
as if the armed school guard didn't hide like a
coward
whilst teenagers took bullets for the sake of their
friends
How dare you say we need to make schools a
harder target?
When they shouldn't be a target in the first place
When if they didn't have guns, school shooters
wouldn't exist anyway
How dare you send your prayers and
condolences

when we all know how little you care about
anything
that doesn't concern you and your money
it's all very clear how the NRA is funding
your policies
How dare you have the audacity to continue to
describe guns
as anything but atrocities?
You campaign and you sell them as if it were
your job
As if it weren't your job
to keep your country safe
to keep the children safe.
The children are the future, and now so many
are dead
I hope you know their blood rests on your head
On the burning ginger mangled matt that you try
and pass for hair
How are you still talking about gun possession
and not control?
When far too much blood has already been shed
it's time for a change
the future is coming ow
these children are rising up
and they won't be quietened down
I can promise you that.

It is what it is

You know when you shrug your shoulders, play
it cool and casual, like "I'm not bothered"
I'm basically made of vinyl, everything slips
right off
-of me, like water off a shiny waterproof jacket,
entirely unaffected
And with that comes my most recent mantra
which has basically just been
life - fuck you.
It is what it is, and I'll be just fine.

Except it's me
and it's my mind
and we're not fooling anybody with *that* lie
yes, it is what it is
but I can't help but wonder - what exactly is *it*?

Is it finally getting better after a decade of
depression
except I can't really described it as "better"
because there's no before to compare it with
I was only twelve and lets be honest here
at that age our sense of self wasn't much more

than sticky glitter lip gloss from a hello kitty
tube
which tasted of melted plastic
in all its carcinogenic glory
and a tatty teddy patch tacked onto my sports
direct McKenzie gym bag

So really there's no before
and it's not getting better
maybe it's just getting to 'be'
for the first time in my adult life
and that realisation that I,
a 24 year old adult, have no I-dea
of what a range of emotions is suppose to be like
because all I'm really used to
is mimicking those around me
a sad little clown mime
in my invisible glass box
with a visible smile

Is it that feeling of sitting on the upper deck of a
red bus
with an ad for Dwayne Johnson's latest movie
plastered on the side
sitting at the window seat in the third aisle
opposite the stairs
the realisation washing over me as I stare
at people walking on the high road
that they're all living a life of their own

for whom all I'll ever be is a stranger
on a bus just driving by

Is it finding myself in a busy room
with people I'd have never thought I'd be
friends with
The jocks and the intimidatingly pretty girls
all here, celebrating my birthday
reminding me to focus on this game that we're
playing from a well loved deck of cards
and I haven't lived in London in almost 2 years
and kind of miss the red buses
but it's okay because this group right here has
forever changed the meaning of riding a bus
and I can't help but smile at the fact that future
me
will smile every time she gets on a bus
thinking about these evenings of parties
and finally having some fun

Is it lying on the soft cream sofa that I've come
to dislike
in the living room that is more lived in now
than it ever was whilst
I was growing up
Laying on the sofa with my head in my mums
lap

watching a 50-something-year-old Shahrukh
Khan refusing to give up his youth and running
in fields with actresses half his age
laying on the sofa with my cat asleep next to me
wondering why on Earth did I ever want to leave
the ones who love me the most
the ones who had tears in their eyes, glistening
with pride
as they bought me my favourite blackforest cake
saying congratulations Dr Siddiqui
you've made it.

Wondering when it was that I made the decision
to move away
knowing how much happier they would be
if I had just stayed
until the moment when my sister makes a
comment
and it turns into a lecture
with yet another pushed agenda
with me somehow pulled into the centre
always expected to be the mediator
and then I'm just crying
emotionally drained and exhausted
on a fun family movie night.

Is it still having days so dark
with clouds so heavy they sink down
and form a fog all around me

a smog so hazy that no matter how hard I try to
remember
about the good days, the better days where I'm
learning to be
and instead I just find myself back in bed
hot and hungry
unshowered and unsightly
alone and lonely

Or is it standing in a beige kitchen in my home
away from home
with freshly cut tulips I received in a city now
two hours away
placing them into a vase I'd brought from home
a vase I'd already filled to the brim with water
so much so that it spilled over, the water icy cold
on my skin
realising that once again I might be feeling
better enough
to not want to cry over spilled drink

I haven't yet figured it out and I don't know that
I ever will
but I tell myself that it's all okay
I'm all cool and casual and don't care enough to
give it that much thought
Can't you tell?

"You've changed"

"You've changed"
The phrase which is every year 6
child's idea of fail-ure
Feeling like it doesn't get much better
than this,
We plaster year books and once-white polo
shirts
With the same phrase
'You're awesome, don't ever change'

And yes, year 6 was probably the last time
I was such a big fish in a small pond
(more accurately – I was tiny, my
puberty-induced growth spurt was still a while
away)
But surely no matter the size,
Fish would much rather change and go swim in
the open sea
Unstifled by pond walls and free from
man-made fish feed.

But honestly, hearing those words now
Especially from those who know me well
Is a moment I happily welcome and treasure
Given that I'm now old enough

Or have lived enough
To appreciate it for what it's meant to be
An acknowledgement of how far I've come and
what I've seen.

Tell me I've changed
because it means that I know what happy feels
like
Tell me I've changed
because it means I can genuinely smile now
Tell me I've changed
because it means that working really fucking
hard at undoing childhood trauma and cultural
dogmas is finally paying off
Tell me I've changed
because it means I'm a better daughter now
Tell me I've changed
because it means I understand how to look after
others without it destroying me
Tell me I've changed
because it means I've dismantled the toxic idea
that looking after me is selfish and ugly
and have managed to relabel selfish a good
seven letter word
Tell me I've changed
because the last thing I'd want, is for younger
me to have lived the experiences she did
without anything to show for it

I want to have changed
And I want to keep changing, growing
Into a better human being

There truly are no words to describe how it feels
To look in the mirror and tell the person looking
back at me
The one who thought that things would never
change
And the darkness would never lift
That it would always be the same
That things did get better, and that we did
change.

Happiness

It may seem impossible right now
but it's true, true what they say
that small moments of happiness
will find their way
creep into your life
almost unnoticed
almost too small
but you'll be there, waiting,
welcoming her with open arms
"it's been a long while" you'll say
as the two of you stroll along.

You notice that happiness looks different now
Different than what you expected
over the years, she's grown into safety
her clothes screaming comfort
instead of the laughter you had anticipated
you see that she no longer
wear the shoes of excitement and loud chatter
instead, they've transformed into sandals
that stay silent
she doesn't wear watches
doesn't have time for time she says

and it's true - the longer she extends her stay
the more you lose track of time
and it's strange because you thought she'd be
punctual
come and go as the situation required
but she seems to stay at the strangest times
offering you reassurance.

Happiness is friendly, too,
you see her walking beside your friends as they
travel
and couples who are spending time together
she blows bubbles in the midst of children
playing
and she sits, present but subdued, when someone
is reminiscing.

And now it seems she has befriended you
a unlikely alliance as far as you're concerned
but then it starts to dawn on you
you realise happiness is different now,
but so are you.